AEP-2315
M-41
$19.98

Children's Dept.

Celebrating
Christmas

By: Shelly Nielsen
Illustrated by: Marie-Claude Monchaux

Published by Abdo & Daughters, 6535 Cecilia Circle, Edina, Minnesota 55439.

Library bound edition distributed by Rockbottom Books, Pentagon Tower, P.O. Box 36036, Minneapolis, Minnesota 55435.

Copyright © 1992 by Abdo Consulting Group, Inc., Pentagon Tower, P.O. Box 36036, Minneapolis, Minnesota 55435. International copyrights reserved in all countries. No part of this book may be reproduced in any form without written permission from the publisher. Printed in the United States.

Edited by: Rosemary Wallner

LIBRARY OF CONGRESS CATALOGING-IN-PUBLICATION DATA

Nielsen, Shelly, 1958-
   Christmas / written by Shelly Nielsen; [edited by Rosemary Wallner]
   p. cm. -- (Holiday celebrations)
   Summary: Rhyming text introduces aspects of this important Christian holiday.
   ISBN 1-56239-067-8
   1. Christmas--Juvenile literature. [1. Christmas.] I. Wallner, Rosemary, 1964- II. Title. III. Series: Nielsen, Shelly, 1958- Holiday celebrations.
GT4985.N54   1992   392.2'68282--dc20   91-73034

International Standard
Book Number:
1-56239-067-8

Library of Congress
Catalog Card Number:
91-73034

Celebrating Christmas

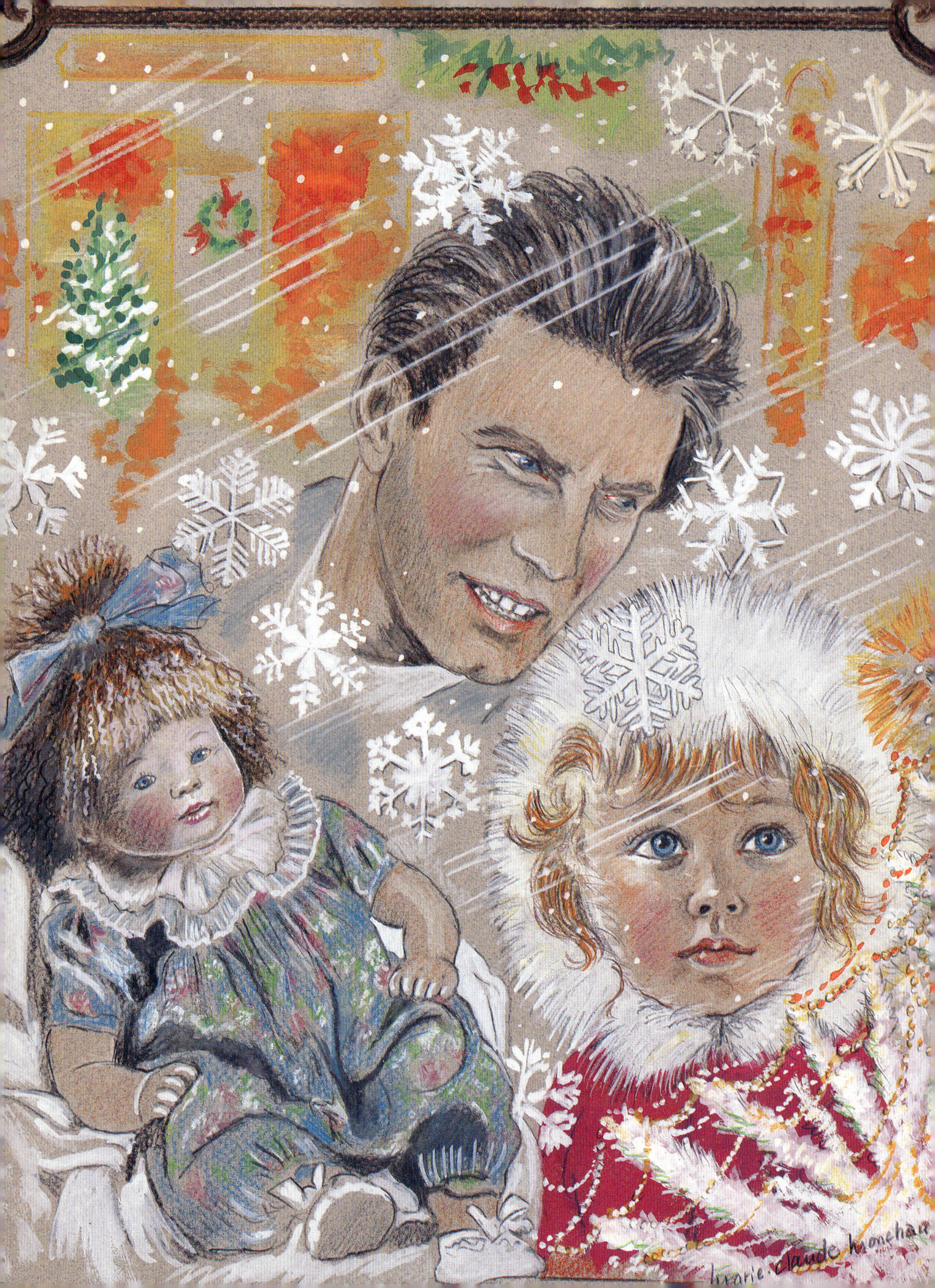
Marie-claude Monchaux

Christmas? Already?

Hey! Look over there!
Christmas decorations, everywhere!
All the shops are wrapped in lights —
green and red, blinking bright.
Daddy looks and shakes his head.
"Christmas? Already? Can't be!" he says.
But I love presents, ribbons, and wreaths.
Christmas is *never* too early for me.

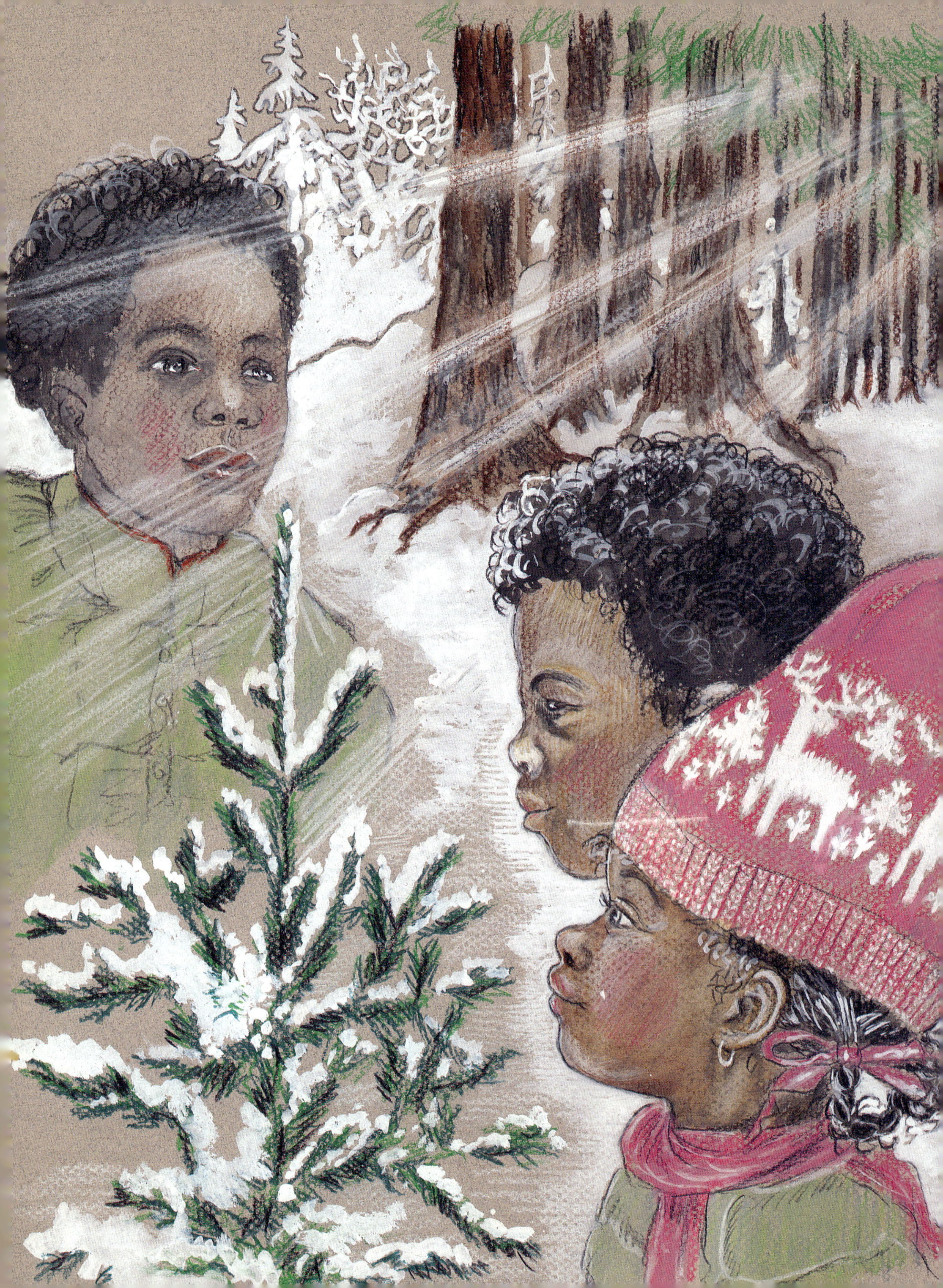

The Best Tree, Ever

Over here —
come quick and see!
I found the perfect Christmas tree.
Imagine how merry it will be
when we dress it in tinsel
and bright, red cranberries!

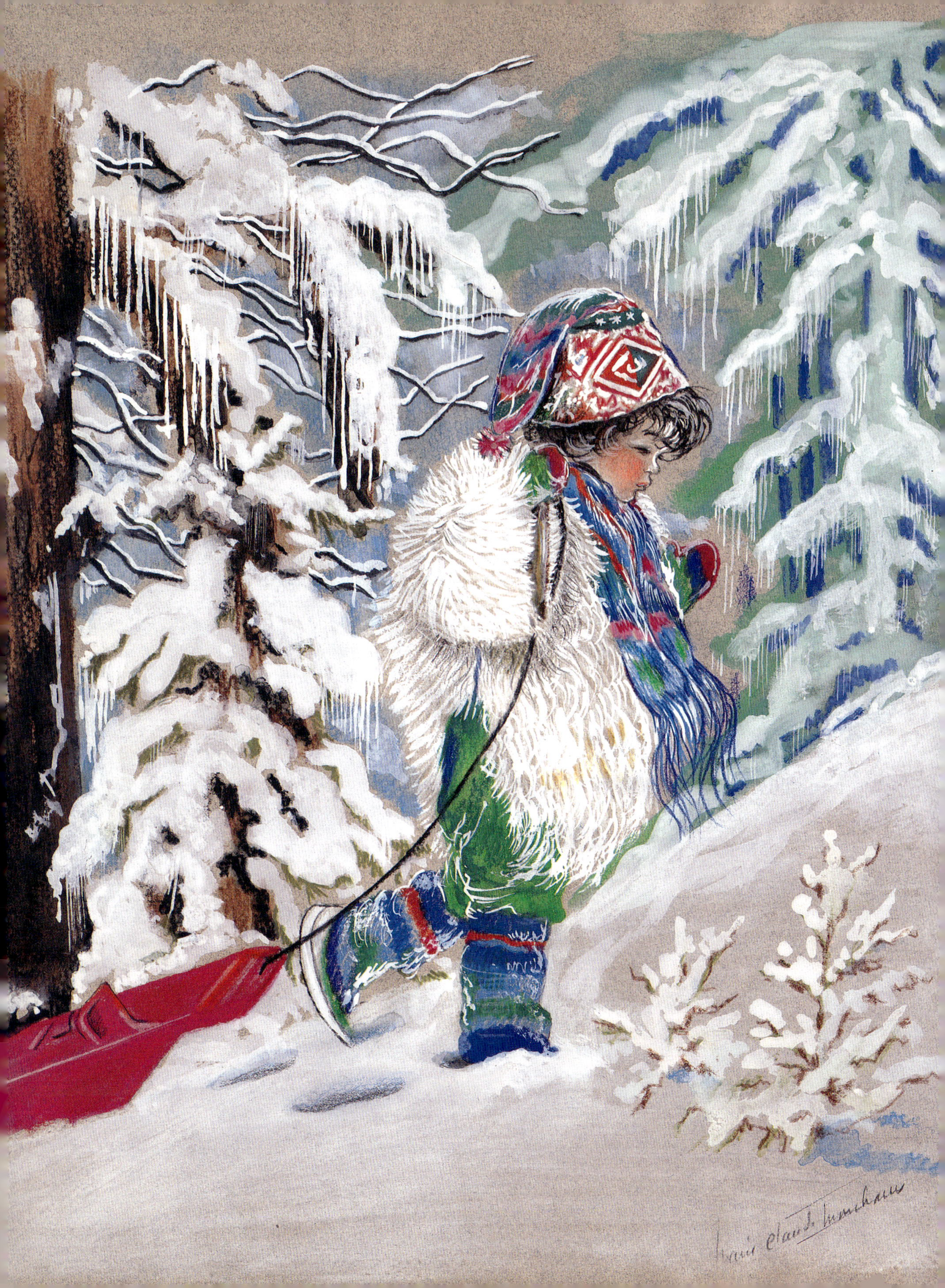

Sled Ride

Squeal!
Slide!
Zip!
Glide!
Sled the curvy hill!
Bump!
Bounce!
Ker-plunk!
Jounce!
Whoops — a snowy spill!

Marie-Claude Monchaux

To My Friends

I helped Mom send Christmas cards.
My job wasn't very hard —
licking stamps and standing on tip-toe
to mail a handful of envelopes.
There they go!
It's fun to say hello
at Christmas.

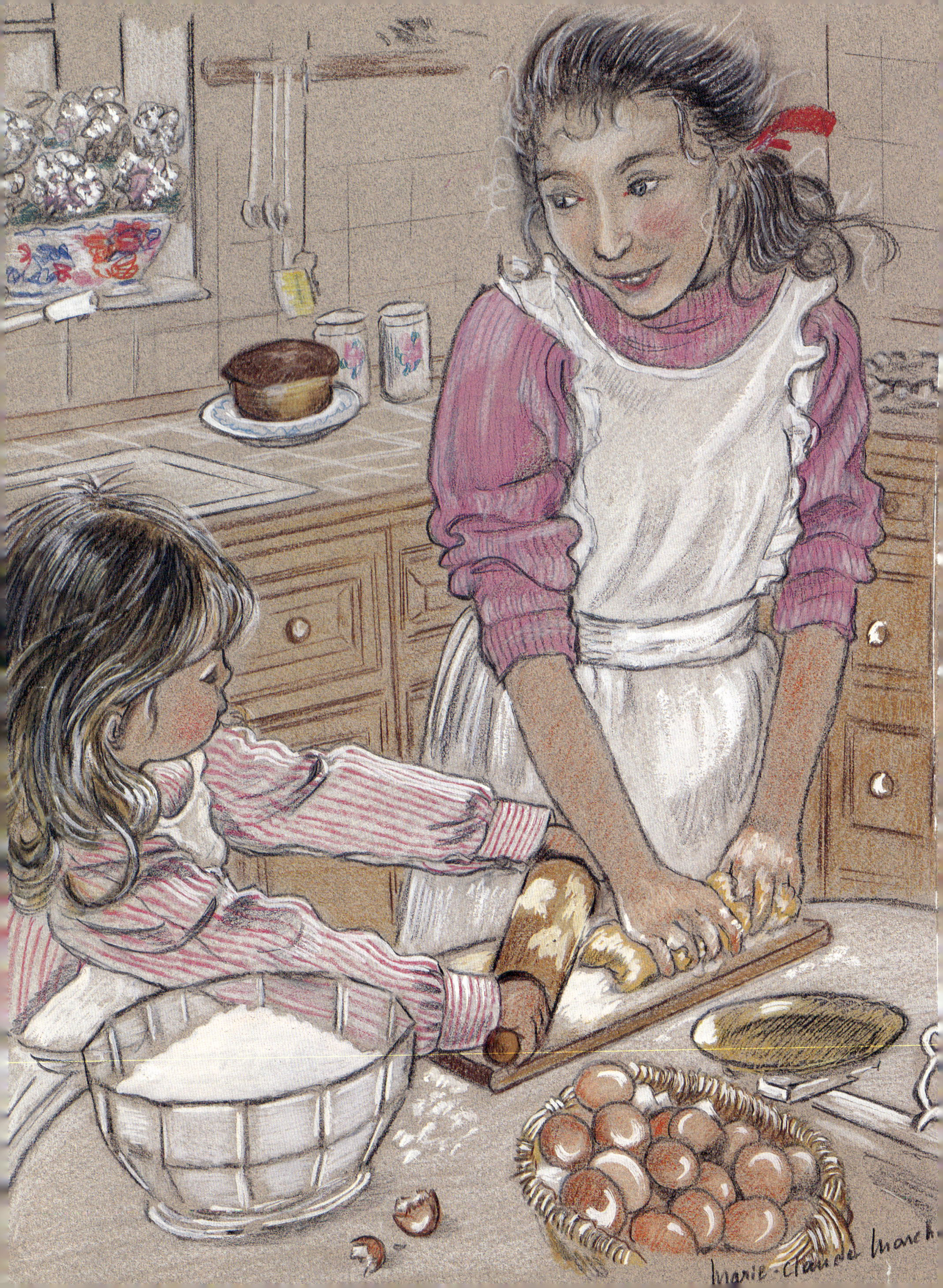
Marie-Claude March

Treats to Eat

Let's make
cookie batter
with flour, eggs,
sugar, and butter.
First, roll the dough good and thin
and cut out skinny gingerbread men.
Now slide them in the oven
and bake till done.
Mmmm . . .
Have one!

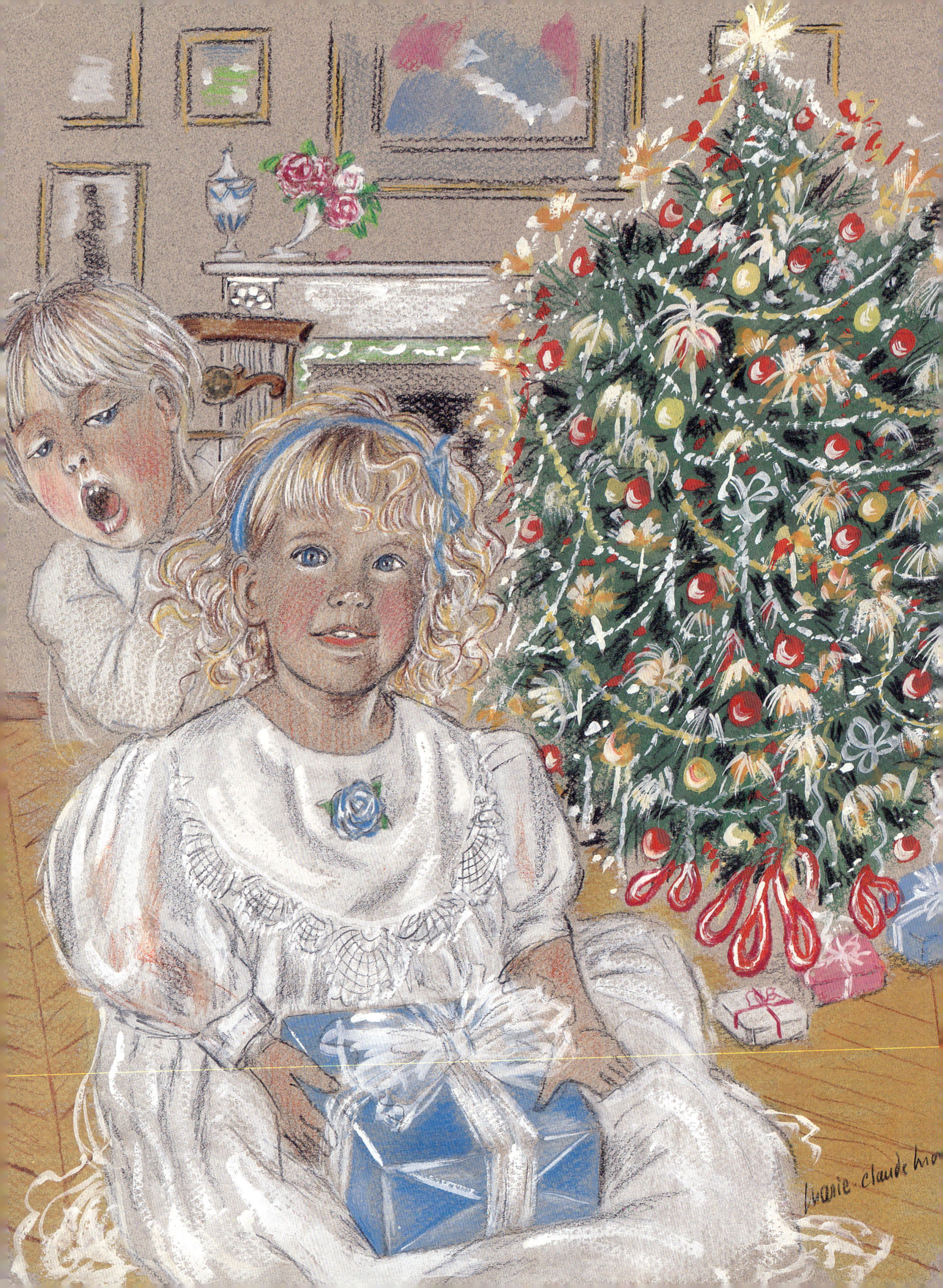

Presents!

Don't snoop!
This present wrapped in blue
is a secret
I picked out just for you.
Would you believe
that a present given
is as fun
as one received?

marie-claude monchaux

Oh, No! Mistletoe!

If you must know,
Grandma gave me a big, fat kiss
under the mistletoe.

I didn't fuss
or cause a ruckus.
After all,
it's Christmas!

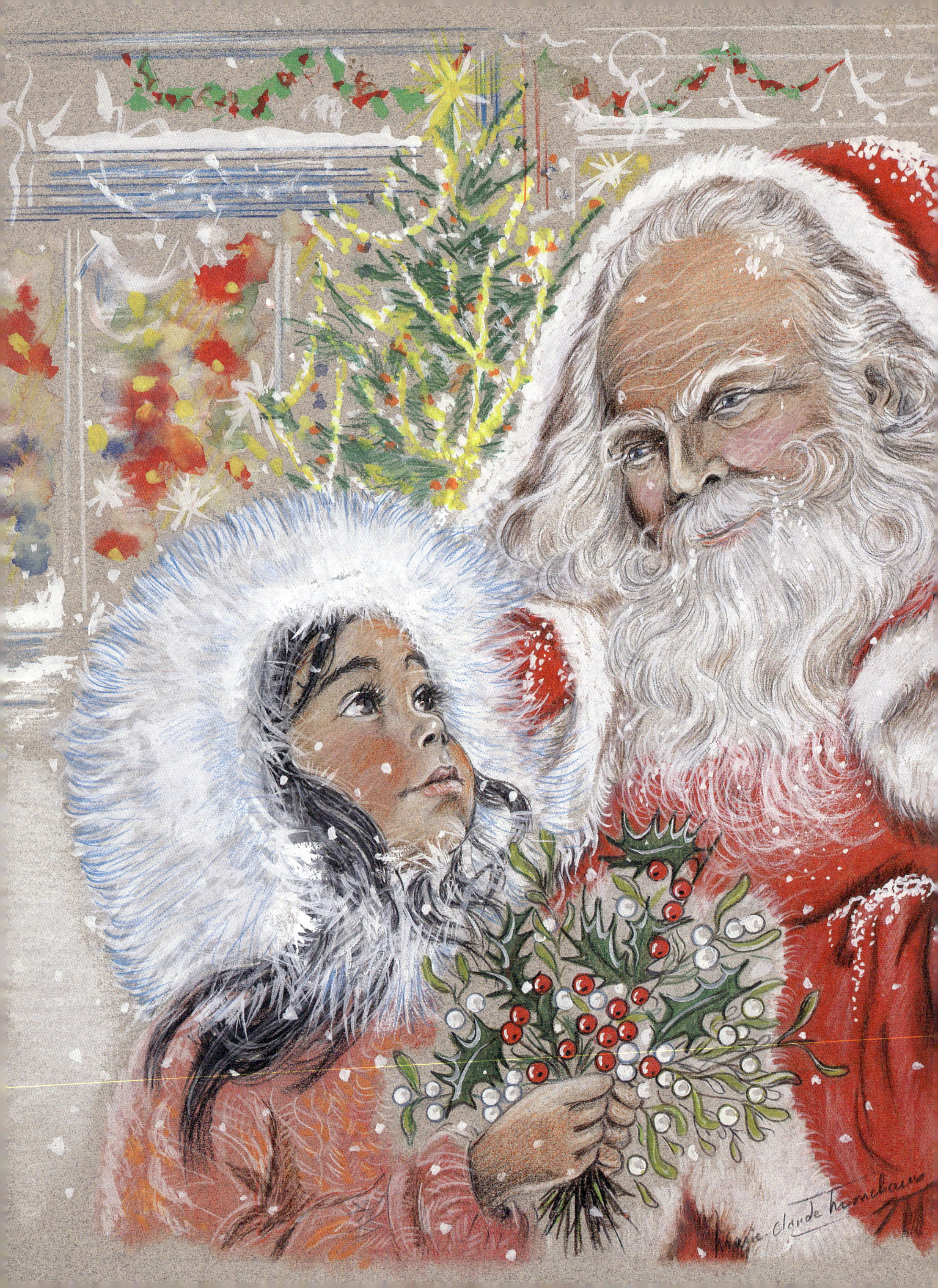

Hello, Santa Claus

I'm next in line
and I'm not scared
of the funny guy in the long, white beard.
    But he's so big
        when I get up close
        that I say to Mom, "Can we go home?"
Just then Santa lifts me
to his high-up lap.
He's so big and fat, he makes me laugh.

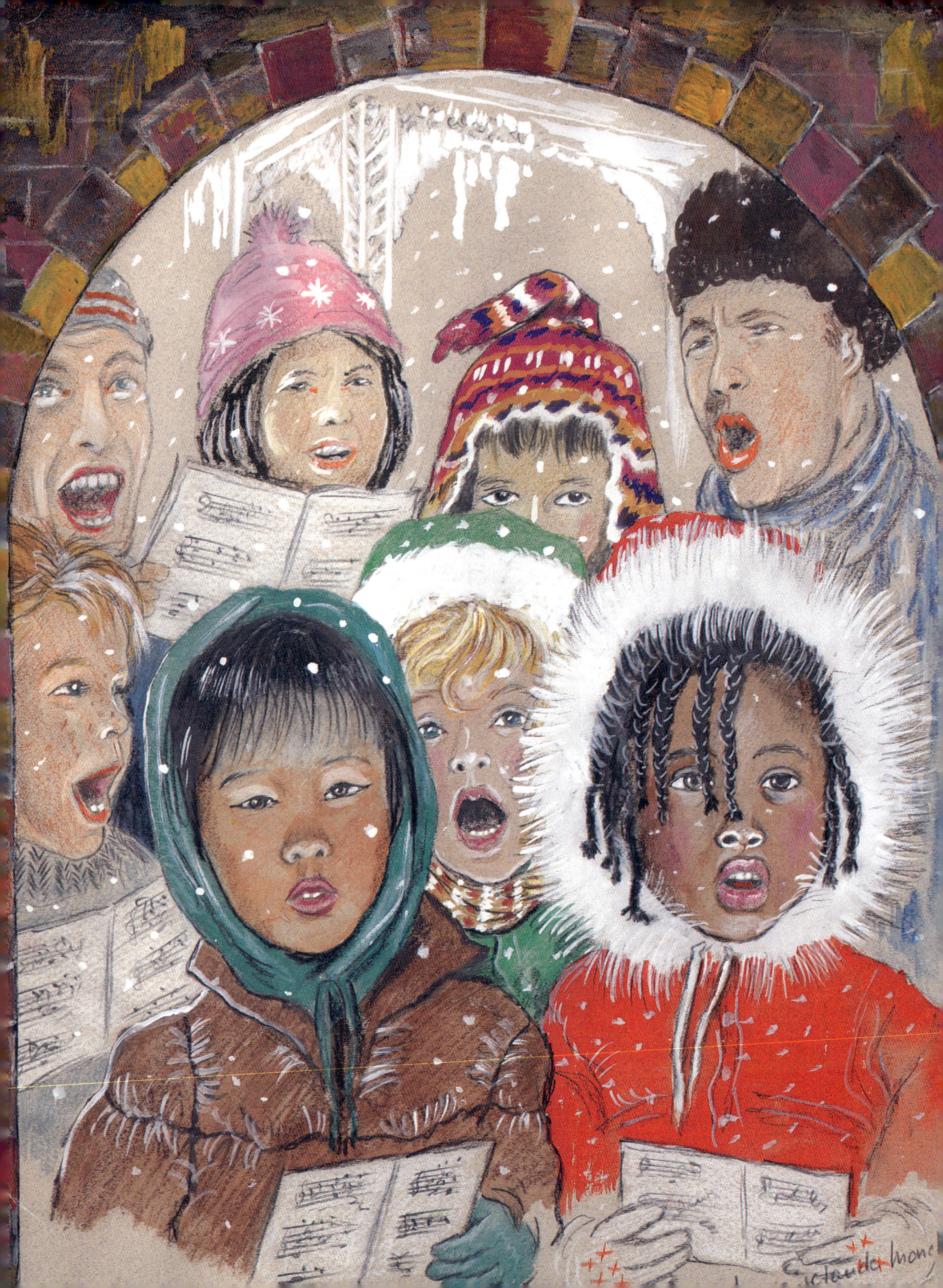

Come Caroling

Come out, come out,
come caroling.
It isn't hard to do.
Put on your mittens, coat, and boots,
and maybe earmuffs, too.
We'll trudge from house to house, my friend.
The wind will howl along.
And though we're frozen to our toes,
we'll sing a cheerful song.

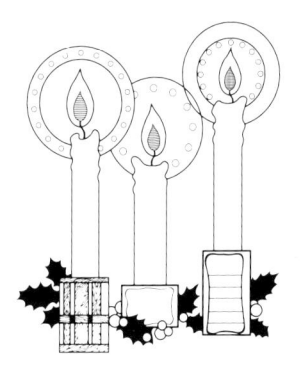

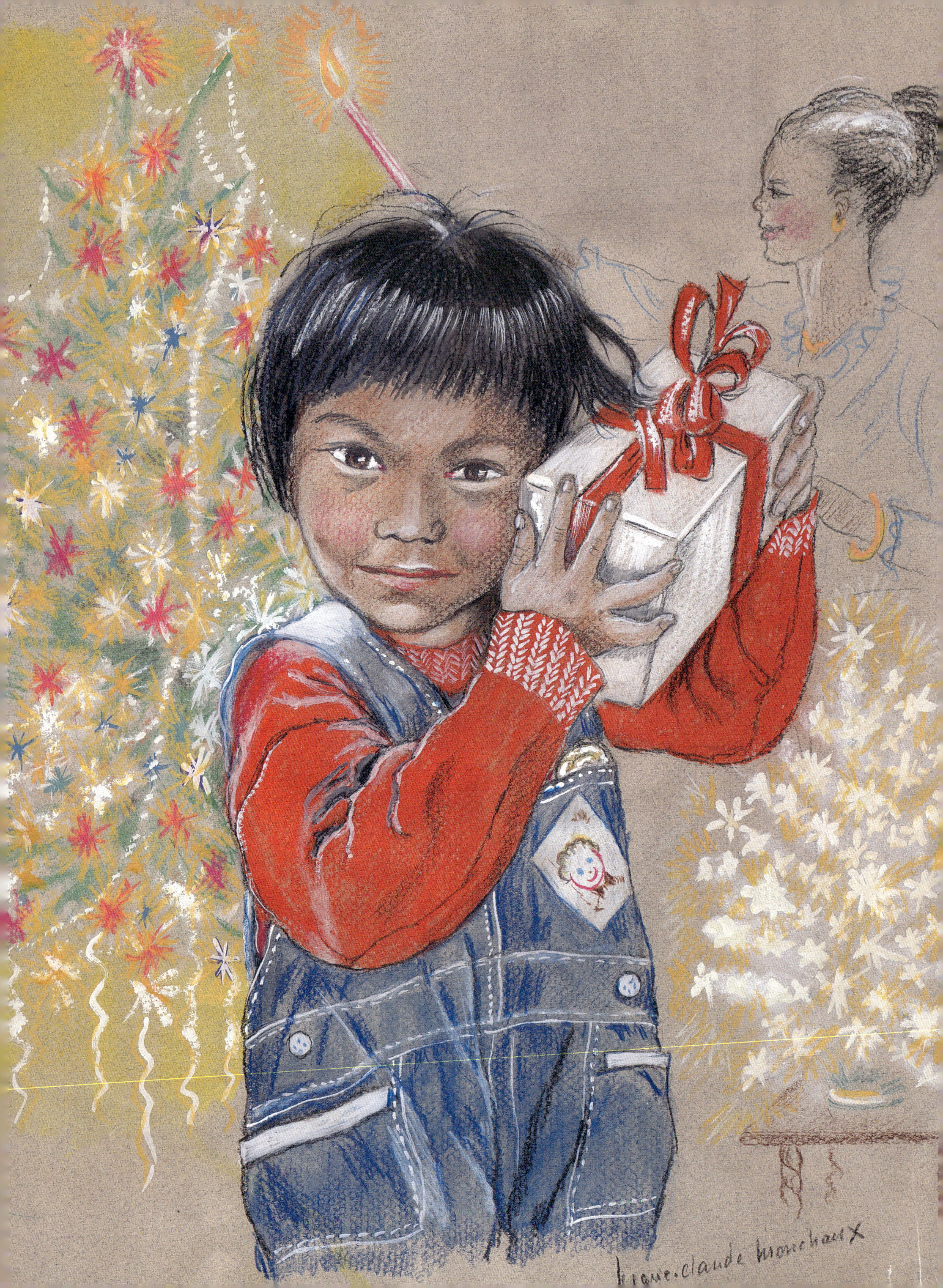
Marie-claude Monchaux

Shake! Shake! Shake!

When I shake my present
something inside
rattles,
rolls,
clatters,
and collides.
What could it be?
What will I get?
A game?
A doll?
An airplane kit?
   Don't ask me;
   I don't know.
   I just hope it's not clothes!

The Night Before Christmas
Clement Moore
ARTHUR
The Night Before Christmas

Story Time

I sip my mug of cocoa
while the fire crackles and glows.
Grandpa is telling a story
with his voice rumbling low.
"'Twas the night before Christmas,"
Grandpa says with a grin.
He knows at the end of the story,
I'll say, "Start all over again."

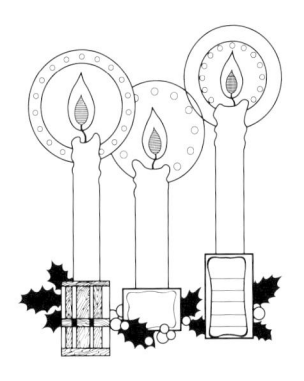

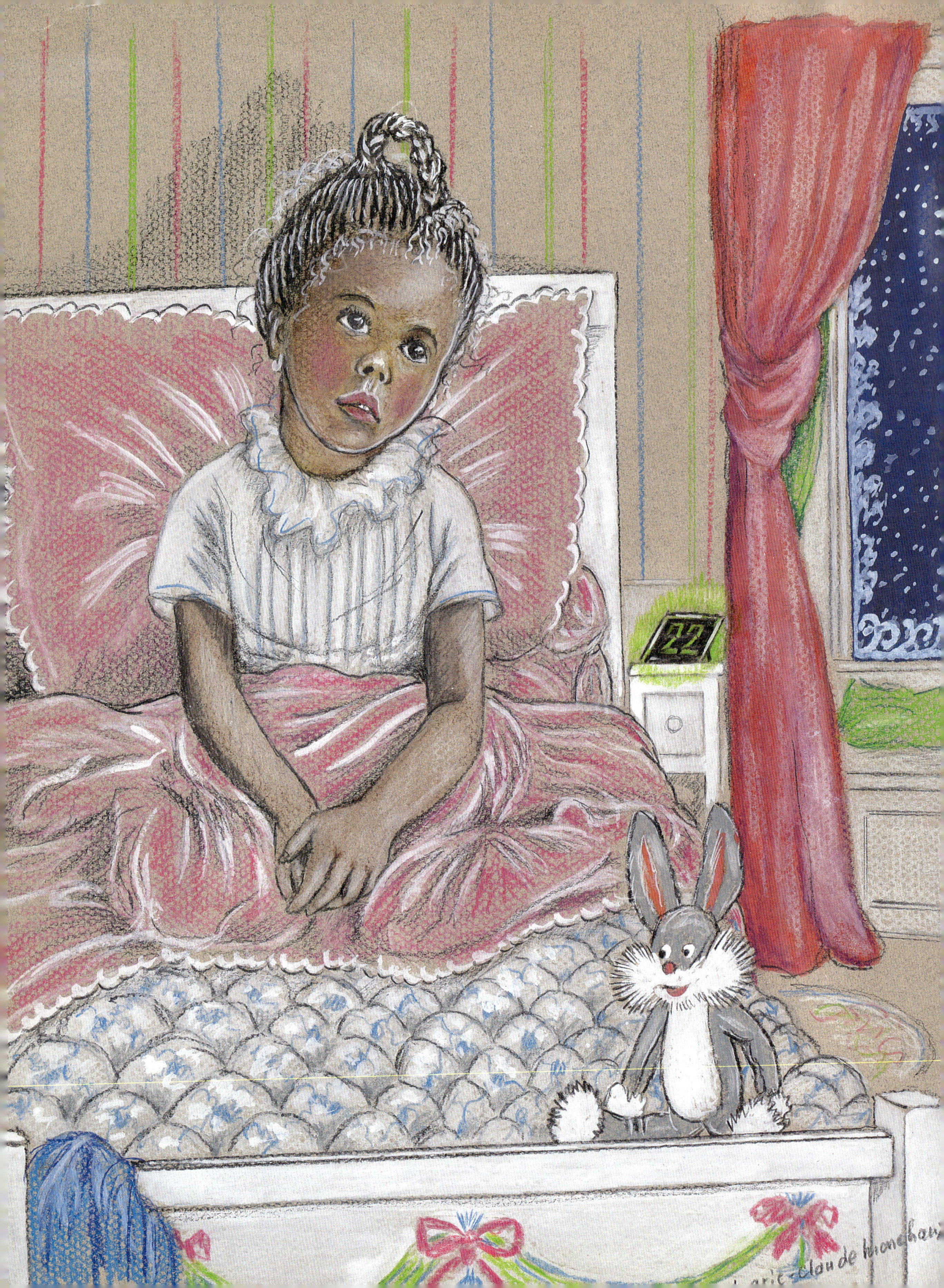

Christmas Eve

On Christmas Eve, Mama said,
"Sleep tight; lay quiet in your bed.
Dream all night of sugar plums,
and in the morning Christmas will come!"
But my eyes and legs are wide awake.
How long, I wonder, does Christmas Eve take?

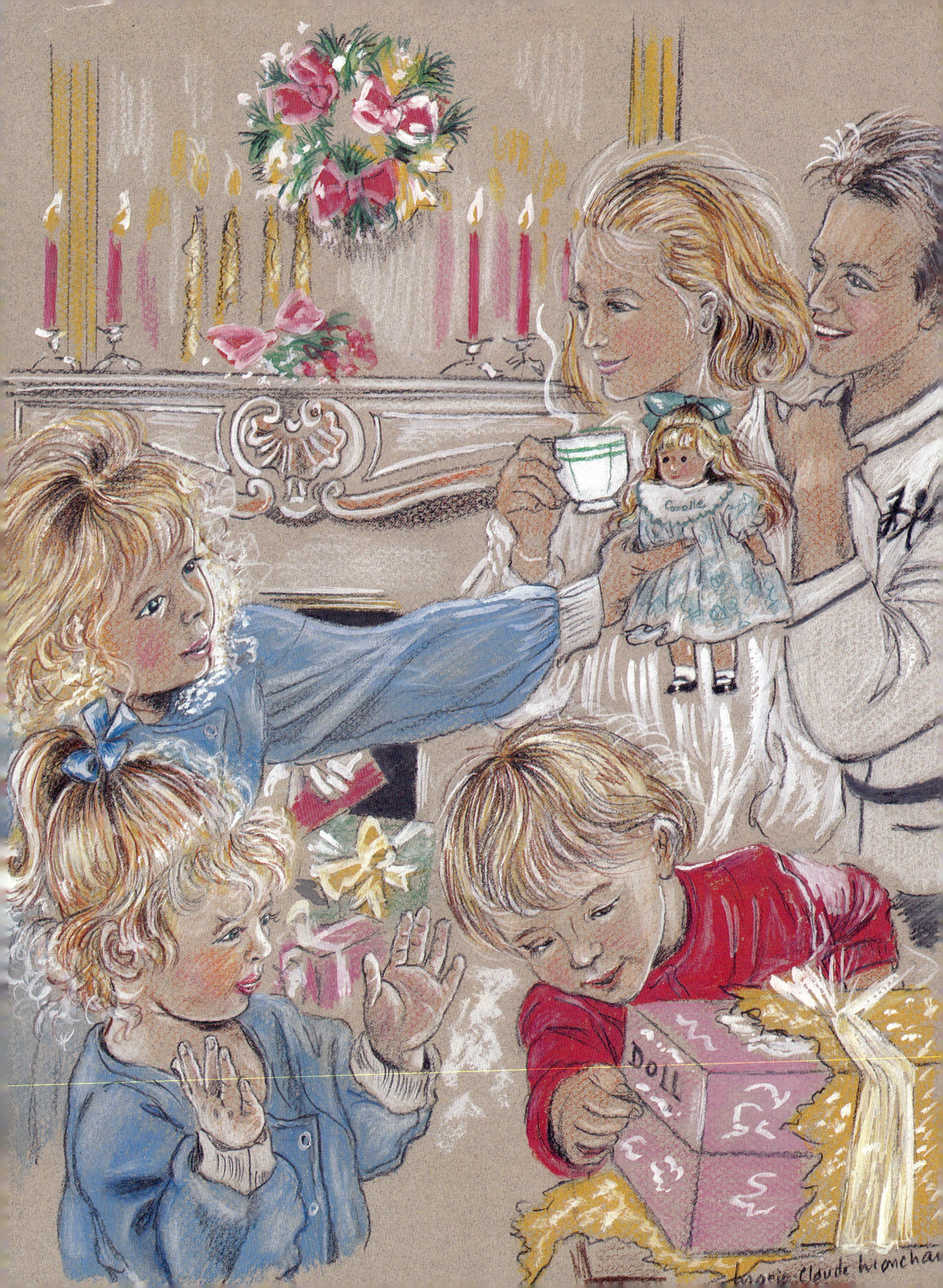
Coralie
DOLL

The Big Day

Psst!
Wake up!
How can you sleep?
It's time to open presents
under the tree.
There's packages for you
and packages for me.
Wake up! It's Christmas — *finally.*

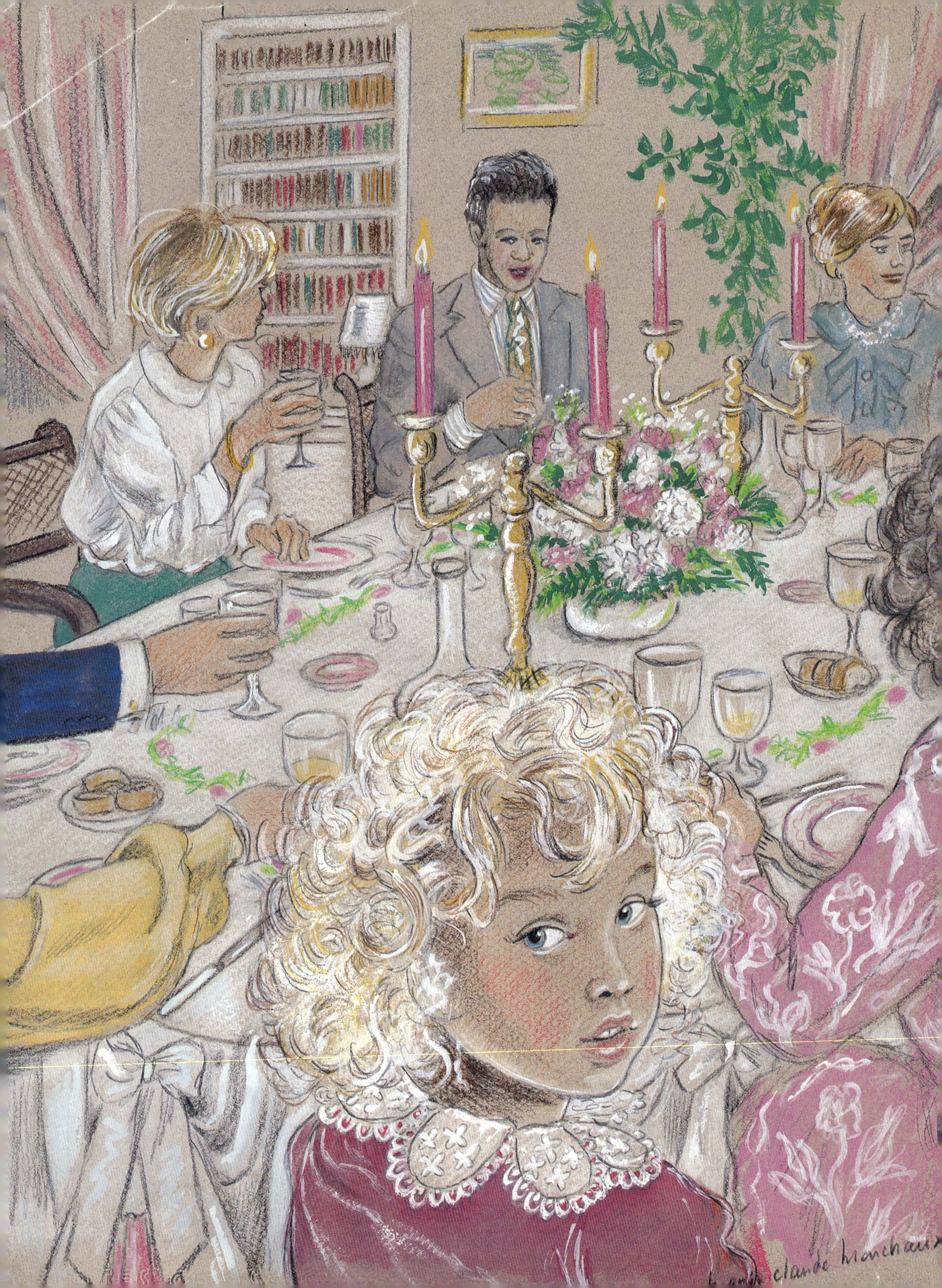

Christmas Feast

Someone special is coming to dinner —
aunts, uncles, and dozens
of cousins.
The whole house smells good
with Christmas food —
ham, potatoes, and muffins.